# Preface

Welcome to the world of stock market investing, where opportunities abound for those who are willing to take the risks and put in the effort to succeed. The stock market can be a confusing and intimidating place for beginners, but with the right knowledge and guidance, anyone can learn to navigate the market and make sound investment decisions.

This ebook is designed to provide you with a comprehensive overview of stock market investing, from the basics of how the market works to advanced strategies for maximizing your returns. Whether you're a complete novice or an experienced investor looking to hone your skills, this ebook has something for you.

Throughout the following pages, we will cover topics such as the different types of stocks, the factors that affect stock prices, fundamentals of stock analysis, and strategies for stock investing for your portfolio. We will also explore various investment strategies, such as value investing, growth investing, and income investing, and provide insights into the risks and rewards of each approach.

Our goal with this ebook is to demystify the stock market and empower you with the knowledge and tools you need to make informed investment decisions. We believe that anyone can succeed in the stock market if they are willing to learn, practice, and stay disciplined in their approach.

So, whether you're looking to invest for the long-term or to make quick gains in the short-term, we hope this ebook will provide you with the guidance and confidence you need to succeed. Let's get started!

# Table of contents

# Chapter 1: Introduction

In this chapter we will cover the following topics:

- *What is stock investing*
- *Why invest in stocks*
- *The benefits and risks of stock investing*
- *Basic concepts of stock investing*
- *The role of stock investing in your financial goals*

### What is stock investing

In this section, we will define what stock investing is and explore how stocks work as an investment. We will also compare stock investing to other investment options, such as bonds and real estate, to help you understand the unique benefits of investing in stocks.

Stock investing refers to the process of buying and selling shares of ownership in a company, known as stocks or equities, with the goal of making a profit. When you purchase a stock, you become a part-owner of the company and have a claim on a portion of its assets and earnings. Stock investing can be done in many ways, such as buying individual stocks or investing in a mutual fund or exchange-traded fund (ETF) that holds a basket of stocks. It is important to note that investing in stocks involves a certain level of risk, as stock prices can be volatile and subject to fluctuations based on various factors.

Compared to other investment options, such as bonds or real estate, stocks are generally considered to offer the potential for higher returns over the long-term. However, they also come with higher levels of risk and volatility.

Overall, stock investing can be a powerful tool for building long-term wealth and achieving your financial goals, but it requires careful consideration and a solid understanding of the risks and rewards involved.

### Why invest in stocks

Here, we will discuss the benefits of investing in stocks, including the potential for high returns and the ability to build long-term wealth. We will also examine the historical returns of stocks and explore how they have outperformed other asset classes over time. Finally, we will discuss the impact of inflation on stocks and how investing in stocks can help you protect your purchasing power over time.

Stocks have historically been a popular investment option, and for good reason. Here are some of the key benefits of investing in stocks:

a) Potential for high returns: Stocks have historically delivered higher returns than other asset classes, such as bonds or real estate. While past performance does not guarantee future results, investing in a diversified portfolio of stocks has the potential to provide significant long-term growth.

b) Protection against inflation: Inflation is the gradual increase in the price of goods and services over time. Stocks have historically provided a hedge against inflation, as the earnings and dividends of companies tend to increase over time as well.

c) Diversification: Investing in stocks allows you to diversify your portfolio and spread your risk across a range of companies and industries. This can help to reduce your overall risk and protect your portfolio from the impact of any single company's performance.

d) Liquidity: Stocks are a highly liquid asset, meaning that they can be easily bought and sold on public stock exchanges. This provides investors with the flexibility to adjust their portfolios as needed and respond to changing market conditions.

**Table 1: Return of various asset class per year**

| Asset Class | Long-Term Return (Approximate) |
| --- | --- |
| Stocks | 7% - 10% per year |
| Bonds | 3% - 5% per year |
| Real Estate | 5% - 7% per year |

However, it's important to note that investing in stocks also comes with certain risks. The value of your investments can fluctuate based on various factors, such as changes in the overall economy or company-specific news. As with any investment, it's important to carefully consider your risk tolerance and investment goals before investing in stocks.

### *The benefits and risks of stock investing*

In this section, we will examine the advantages of investing in stocks, including the potential for high returns and the ability to build a diversified portfolio. However, we will also discuss the risks associated with investing in stocks, including market volatility, company-specific risks, and other economic and political risks. We will also explore strategies for managing these risks.

Benefits of stock investing:

a) Potential for high returns: Stocks have historically delivered higher returns than other asset classes, such as bonds or real estate. This potential for high returns is a major draw for investors.

b) Diversification: Investing in stocks allows you to diversify your portfolio and spread your risk across a range of companies and industries. This can help to reduce your overall risk and protect your portfolio from the impact of any single company's performance.

c) Liquidity: Stocks are a highly liquid asset, meaning that they can be easily bought and sold on public stock exchanges. This provides investors with the flexibility to adjust their portfolios as needed and respond to changing market conditions.

d) Ownership: Investing in stocks gives you a stake in the ownership of the companies you invest in. This can provide a sense of pride and satisfaction, as well as the opportunity to vote on important issues at shareholder meetings.

Risks of stock investing:

a) Volatility: Stock prices can be highly volatile, meaning they can fluctuate widely in response to changes in the overall economy or company-specific news. This can lead to significant short-term losses, which can be difficult for some investors to handle.

b) Company-specific risks: Investing in individual stocks carries the risk of company-specific events, such as a decline in sales or a change in management, which can negatively impact the stock price.

c) Economic and political risks: Changes in the overall economy or political environment can have a significant impact on stock prices. For example, a recession or trade war can lead to widespread declines in stock prices.

d) Potential for fraud: While rare, there is always the risk of fraudulent activities, such as accounting fraud, which can negatively impact the value of your investments.

Overall, investing in stocks offers the potential for high returns and diversification, but it's important to carefully consider the risks involved and develop a solid investment strategy that aligns with your goals and risk tolerance.

### *Basic concepts of stock investing*

Here, we will cover the fundamental concepts of stock investing, including what a stock is and how it works. We will also discuss the different types of stocks and their characteristics, such as common stock and preferred stock. Additionally, we will cover stock market indexes and their role in investing, as well as how companies issue stocks and how investors buy and sell them.

Before diving into stock investing, it's important to have a basic understanding of some key concepts. Here are some of the most important terms to know:

a) Stock: A stock, also known as a share or equity, represents ownership in a company. When you buy a stock, you become a part-owner of the company and are entitled to a portion of its earnings and assets.

b) Stock exchange: A stock exchange is a marketplace where stocks and other securities are bought and sold. Examples include the New York Stock Exchange (NYSE) and the Nasdaq.

c) Index: An index is a benchmark that tracks the performance of a group of stocks. Examples include the S&P 500 and the Dow Jones Industrial Average.

d) Broker: A broker is a person or company that acts as an intermediary between buyers and sellers of securities. Brokers can help you buy and sell stocks and may also provide investment advice and other services.

e) Portfolio: A portfolio is a collection of investments, such as stocks, bonds, and mutual funds, held by an investor.

f) Dividend: A dividend is a payment made by a company to its shareholders, usually in the form of cash or additional shares of stock. Dividends are typically paid out of a company's earnings.

g) Capital gains: Capital gains refer to the profit earned from selling a stock for more than its purchase price.

h) Risk: Risk refers to the potential for loss or volatility associated with an investment. All investments carry some level of risk, and it's important to carefully consider your risk tolerance before investing in stocks.

Understanding these basic concepts is essential for anyone looking to invest in stocks. As you gain more experience and knowledge, you can begin to explore more advanced concepts and strategies for investing.

### *The role of stock investing in your financial goals*

In this section, we will explore how stock investing fits into your overall financial plan. We will discuss the importance of setting realistic expectations for stock investing returns and developing a long-term investment strategy with stocks. Finally, we will examine how stock investing can help you achieve your financial goals, such as saving for retirement or building wealth for future generations.

Stock investing can play an important role in achieving your financial goals. Here are some ways that stock investing can help you reach your financial objectives:

a) Building wealth: Stock investing can be an effective way to build wealth over the long-term. Historically, stocks have delivered higher returns than other asset classes, such as bonds or real estate. By investing in a diversified portfolio of stocks, you can potentially earn high returns and build wealth over time.

b) Saving for retirement: Investing in stocks is a common strategy for saving for retirement. By investing in a tax-advantaged retirement account, such as an IRA or 401(k), you can take advantage of compounding returns and potentially grow your retirement savings over time.

c) Achieving financial independence: Investing in stocks can help you achieve financial independence by providing a source of passive income. By building a portfolio of dividend-paying stocks, you can potentially earn regular income without having to work a traditional job.

d) Funding other financial goals: Investing in stocks can also provide a source of funding for other financial goals, such as paying for a child's education or buying a house. By investing in a diversified portfolio of stocks, you can potentially earn high returns and build wealth that can be used to achieve your other financial goals.

However, it's important to remember that stock investing comes with risks, and it's not a guarantee of success. Before investing in stocks, it's important to carefully consider your goals, risk tolerance, and investment strategy. By developing a solid plan and staying disciplined, you can potentially achieve your financial objectives through stock investing.

In this chapter we will cover the following topics:

- *How the stock market works*
- *Types of stocks and investment vehicles*
- *Major stock exchanges and indices*
- *Factors that affect stock prices*
- *Market trends and cycles*

### How the stock market works

This section provides an overview of the stock market, including what it is, how it functions, and who the major players are. It will also cover topics such as the role of stockbrokers, the importance of market liquidity, and the different types of securities that are traded.

What is the Stock Market?

The stock market is a collection of exchanges and markets where publicly traded companies issue shares to raise capital from investors. Investors purchase these shares in the hopes of earning a return on their investment, either through capital gains (an increase in the stock price) or through dividends (a portion of the company's profits paid out to shareholders). The stock market is often seen as a bellwether for the overall economy. The performance of the stock market can be influenced by a wide range of factors, including economic indicators, geopolitical events, and corporate earnings reports.

How Does the Stock Market Function?

The stock market functions as a marketplace where buyers and sellers come together to trade shares of publicly traded companies. The market is facilitated by brokers, who act as intermediaries between buyers and sellers. When a company decides to go public, it issues shares of stock in an initial public offering (IPO). Investors can then purchase these shares through a stockbroker or an online trading platform. Once a stock is publicly traded, its price is determined by the forces of supply and demand.

The price of a stock can fluctuate based on a variety of factors, including the performance of the company, the broader economy, and investor sentiment. Investors can buy and sell shares of stock at any time, but the price they pay will depend on the current market price of the stock.

Who are the Major Players in the Stock Market?

The stock market is made up of a variety of players, including individual investors, institutional investors, brokers, and market makers. Individual investors are people who buy and sell stocks on their own behalf. They may do this through a broker or by using an online trading platform. Institutional investors are organizations that manage large sums of money on behalf of clients such as pension funds, mutual funds, and hedge funds. They may also buy and sell stocks on their own behalf. Brokers are individuals or firms that facilitate trades between buyers and sellers. They may work for a brokerage firm or operate as independent brokers. Market makers are firms that facilitate trades by buying and selling stocks on their own behalf. They help ensure that there is always a buyer or seller available for a particular stock.

Stockbrokers play a vital role in the stock market by facilitating trades between buyers and sellers. They act as intermediaries, executing trades on behalf of their clients and providing guidance and advice on investment decisions. Stockbrokers can be either full-service or discount brokers. Full-service brokers offer a range of investment services, including research and analysis, portfolio management, and financial planning. Discount brokers, on the other hand, offer limited services and focus mainly on executing trades at a lower cost.

### *Types of stocks and investment vehicles*

This section explores the different types of stocks that are available to investors, including common stocks, preferred stocks, and exchange-traded funds (ETFs). It will also cover other investment vehicles such as bonds, mutual funds, and options. There are several types of stocks and investment vehicles available for investors to consider when building a diversified portfolio. Here are some of the most common:

Common Stock: This is the most well-known type of stock. When you buy common stock, you become a partial owner of the company and are entitled to vote on certain issues at the company's annual meeting. You may also receive dividends if the company decides to distribute them.

Preferred Stock: This type of stock is different from common stock in that it typically pays a fixed dividend and has priority over common stock in the event of bankruptcy or liquidation.

Bonds: A bond is a loan made by an investor to a company or government entity. In exchange for the loan, the borrower pays the investor interest over a set period of time. When the bond matures, the borrower repays the principal.

Exchange-Traded Funds (ETFs): An ETF is a basket of stocks or bonds that are traded on an exchange like a stock. ETFs are designed to track a specific index or sector, and they offer investors a way to diversify their portfolio without having to buy individual stocks or bonds.

Mutual Funds: A mutual fund is a pool of money collected from many investors that is used to purchase a diversified portfolio of stocks, bonds, or other securities. Mutual funds are managed by professional money managers who aim to achieve a specific investment objective.

Real Estate Investment Trusts (REITs): A REIT is a company that owns or finances income-producing real estate, such as apartments, office buildings, and shopping centers. REITs are designed to provide investors with a way to invest in real estate without having to buy physical property.

Options: An option is a contract that gives the holder the right, but not the obligation, to buy or sell an underlying asset at a specific price and time. Options can be used to hedge risk or speculate on price movements in the underlying asset.

Each type of investment vehicle has its own benefits and risks, and investors should carefully consider their investment goals and risk tolerance before making any investment decisions.

### Major stock exchanges and indices

This section provides an overview of the major stock exchanges around the world, including the New York Stock Exchange (NYSE), the NASDAQ, and the Tokyo Stock Exchange. It may also discuss popular stock market indices such as the S&P 500, the Dow Jones Industrial Average, and the Nikkei 225. Major stock exchanges around the world provide a platform for investors to buy and sell stocks and other securities. Here are some of the most prominent stock exchanges and indices:

New York Stock Exchange (NYSE): The NYSE is the largest stock exchange in the world by market capitalization. It lists more than 2,800 companies, including some of the biggest names in finance, technology, and retail.

NASDAQ: The NASDAQ is the second-largest stock exchange in the world by market capitalization. It is known for listing many technology and biotech companies, as well as several large non-U.S. companies.

Tokyo Stock Exchange (TSE): The TSE is the largest stock exchange in Japan and one of the largest in Asia. It lists more than 3,500 companies, including some of the largest Japanese corporations.

London Stock Exchange (LSE): The LSE is one of the oldest and most prestigious stock exchanges in the world. It lists more than 2,700 companies, including many large multinational corporations.

Shanghai Stock Exchange (SSE): The SSE is one of the two major stock exchanges in China. It lists more than 1,500 companies, including many large Chinese state-owned enterprises.

Hong Kong Stock Exchange (HKEX): The HKEX is one of the major stock exchanges in Asia. It lists more than 2,300 companies, including many large Chinese and international corporations.

In addition to these stock exchanges, there are several major indices that investors use to track the performance of the overall stock market or specific sectors. Here are a few of the most well-known indices:

S&P 500: The S&P 500 is a market-cap weighted index of 500 large-cap U.S. stocks. It is widely used as a benchmark for the overall performance of the U.S. stock market.

Dow Jones Industrial Average (DJIA): The DJIA is a price-weighted index of 30 large-cap U.S. stocks. It is one of the oldest and most widely recognized stock market indices.

NASDAQ Composite: The NASDAQ Composite is an index of more than 3,000 stocks listed on the NASDAQ stock exchange. It is known for its heavy weighting in technology and biotech companies.

FTSE 100: The FTSE 100 is an index of 100 large-cap U.K. stocks listed on the LSE. It is widely used as a benchmark for the overall performance of the U.K. stock market.

Nikkei 225: The Nikkei 225 is a price-weighted index of 225 large-cap Japanese stocks listed on the TSE. It is widely used as a benchmark for the overall performance of the Japanese stock market.

These stock exchanges and indices provide investors with a way to track the performance of individual companies, specific sectors, and entire markets. Investors can use this information to make informed investment decisions and build a diversified portfolio.

### *Factors that affect stock prices*

This section examines the various factors that can impact stock prices, including economic indicators, company earnings reports, interest rates, and geopolitical events. Stock prices are determined by a variety of factors that affect the demand and supply of the stock in the market. Understanding these factors is crucial for investors who want to make informed decisions and achieve their investment goals. We will discuss some of the key factors that affect stock prices below:

Economic indicators

Economic indicators such as inflation, interest rates, GDP growth, and employment rates can have a significant impact on stock prices. For example, higher inflation and interest rates tend to reduce consumer spending and business investment, leading to lower earnings for companies and lower stock prices. Conversely, strong GDP growth and low unemployment rates can boost investor confidence and drive stock prices higher.

Company earnings

A company's earnings are one of the most important factors affecting its stock price. If a company's earnings exceed market expectations, its stock price is likely to rise, and vice versa. Investors also pay close attention to a company's revenue growth, profit margins, and earnings guidance to gauge its future prospects.

Market sentiment

Market sentiment refers to the overall mood of investors and their confidence in the market. Positive market sentiment can lead to higher stock prices, while negative sentiment can lead to lower prices. Factors that can influence market sentiment include news events, geopolitical tensions, and investor sentiment indicators such as the volatility index (VIX index).

Industry trends

Stock prices are also influenced by trends and developments in specific industries. For example, technological advances can boost the prices of technology stocks, while regulatory changes or political developments can impact prices in the healthcare or energy sectors.

Company-specific news

News related to a specific company can have a significant impact on its stock price. This can include announcements of new products, mergers and acquisitions, earnings reports, and legal or regulatory issues. Investors need to keep track of such news and its potential impact on the company's future prospects.

Market trends and momentum

Stock prices are also influenced by overall market trends and momentum. This can include short-term trends such as the performance of the broader stock market, as well as longer-term trends such as changes in demographics, consumer behavior, or global economic conditions.

In conclusion, there are many factors that can influence stock prices, and investors need to consider all of them when making investment decisions. By analyzing economic indicators, company earnings, market sentiment, industry trends, company-specific news, and market trends and momentum, investors can gain a deeper understanding of the market and make informed decisions to achieve their investment goals.

### *Market trends and cycles*

This section discusses the cyclical nature of the stock market and how investors can identify market trends and cycles. It will also cover strategies for investing during different phases of the market cycle, such as growth, contraction, and recovery.

The stock market is well known for its cyclical nature, where the prices of stocks and other securities rise and fall in a repeating pattern. These cycles are typically driven by a variety of factors, including economic conditions, market sentiment, and changes in government policy.

There are several key indicators that investors can use to identify market trends and cycles. One of the most popular is the moving average, which is a calculation of the average price of a security over a set period of time. By analyzing the moving average, investors can get a sense of whether a stock or market is trending upward or downward.

Another useful indicator is the relative strength index (RSI), which measures the strength of a security's price movement by comparing its gains to its losses over a given period. The RSI is a valuable tool for identifying overbought and oversold conditions, which can signal potential market reversals.

Investors can also use technical analysis to identify patterns in market trends and cycles. This approach involves analyzing charts and graphs of price movements and looking for recurring patterns that can provide insight into future price movements.

It's important to note that while these indicators and techniques can be helpful in identifying market trends and cycles, they are not foolproof. The stock market is inherently unpredictable, and even the most seasoned investors can be caught off guard by sudden market movements. To achieve success in the stock market, investors need to have a clear understanding of the different phases of the market cycle and develop investment strategies that are appropriate for each phase.

During the growth phase of the market cycle, investors should focus on investing in high-growth stocks that have the potential for significant capital appreciation. These stocks typically outperform the broader market during periods of economic growth and rising corporate earnings. Growth investors should focus on companies that are expanding their market share, introducing new products or services, and generating strong revenue growth.

During the contraction phase of the market cycle, investors should focus on protecting their capital and minimizing their exposure to risk. This is a time when the market experiences a significant decline in value, and investors may see their investments lose value rapidly. To minimize risk, investors should focus on defensive stocks that have historically performed well during economic downturns, such as consumer staples, healthcare, and utilities.

During the recovery phase of the market cycle, investors should focus on investing in undervalued stocks that have the potential for significant capital appreciation as the economy recovers. These stocks typically have strong fundamentals but have been overlooked by the broader market. Investors should focus on companies that are well-positioned to benefit from the economic recovery, such as those in the manufacturing, construction, and technology sectors.

Regardless of the phase of the market cycle, investors should always maintain a diversified portfolio and avoid making emotional decisions based on short-term market movements. By staying disciplined and focused on their long-term investment goals, investors can achieve success in the stock market and build wealth over time.

Ultimately, the key to successful investing in the stock market is to develop a long-term strategy based on solid research and analysis, and to remain disciplined and patient in the face of market volatility. By staying focused on your investment goals and maintaining a diversified portfolio, you can ride out the ups and downs of the market and achieve long-term success.

In this chapter we will cover the following topics:

- *Financial statements and ratios*
- *Valuation methods and techniques*
- *Analyzing industry and market trends*
- *Identifying and assessing risks*

### Financial statements and ratios

Financial statements and ratios are important tools for analyzing stocks and making investment decisions. These documents provide valuable information about a company's financial health, profitability, and future growth prospects. In this section, we will discuss the main types of financial statements and ratios used in stock analysis.

**Financial Statements**

The main types of financial statements are the balance sheet, income statement, and cash flow statement. These documents provide a snapshot of a company's financial position at a particular point in time and its financial performance over a specific period.

Balance Sheet

The balance sheet shows a company's assets, liabilities, and equity at a specific point in time. Assets are what a company owns and can include cash, investments, property, and equipment. Liabilities are what a company owes and can include loans, accounts payable, and taxes owed. Equity is what remains after deducting liabilities from assets and can include retained earnings and stockholder equity.

Income Statement

The income statement shows a company's revenue, expenses, and net income over a specific period. Revenue is what a company earns from selling products or services. Expenses are what a company spends to produce and sell those products or services. Net income is what remains after deducting expenses from revenue.

Cash Flow Statement

The cash flow statement shows a company's cash inflows and outflows over a specific period. Cash inflows can include sales revenue, investments, and loans. Cash outflows can include expenses, investments, and loan payments. The cash flow statement is important because it shows whether a company is generating cash or using cash to finance its operations.

**Financial Ratios**

Financial ratios are calculated using data from the financial statements and are used to analyze a company's financial health, profitability, and future growth prospects. Here are some of the main financial ratios used in stock analysis:

### Price-to-Earnings Ratio (P/E Ratio)

The P/E ratio is calculated by dividing a company's stock price by its earnings per share (EPS). It shows how much investors are willing to pay for each dollar of earnings. A high P/E ratio can indicate that investors expect strong growth in the future, while a low P/E ratio can indicate that investors are not optimistic about the company's growth prospects.

### Price-to-Book Ratio (P/B Ratio)

The P/B ratio is calculated by dividing a company's stock price by its book value per share. Book value is calculated by subtracting a company's liabilities from its assets and dividing the result by the number of outstanding shares. The P/B ratio shows how much investors are willing to pay for each dollar of the company's book value. A high P/B ratio can indicate that investors believe the company's assets are undervalued, while a low P/B ratio can indicate that investors believe the company's assets are overvalued.

### Debt-to-Equity Ratio

The debt-to-equity ratio is calculated by dividing a company's total debt by its total equity. It shows how much debt a company has relative to its equity. A high debt-to-equity ratio can indicate that a company is highly leveraged and may be at risk of defaulting on its debt, while a low debt-to-equity ratio can indicate that a company has a strong financial position.

### Return on Equity (ROE)

ROE is calculated by dividing a company's net income by its total equity. It shows how much profit a company is generating relative to its equity. A high ROE can indicate that a company is profitable and efficient at using its equity to generate income, while a low ROE can indicate that a company is not generating enough profit relative to its equity.

### Current Ratio

This ratio measures a company's liquidity by dividing its current assets by its current liabilities. A high current ratio can indicate that a company has a strong ability to meet its short-term obligations, while a low current ratio can indicate that a company may have difficulty meeting its obligations.

In summary, financial statements and ratios are essential tools for stock analysis. They provide investors with a wealth of information about a company's financial performance, health, and prospects, allowing them to make informed investment decisions.

### *Valuation methods and techniques*

This section discusses about different valuation methods and techniques for stocks and other financial assets. Valuation is the process of determining the fair value of a stock or other asset. Valuation is important for investors because it allows them to determine whether a stock is overvalued or undervalued and make informed investment decisions. There are several methods and techniques that investors use to value stocks. Following are the most commonly used methods and techniques.

Discounted Cash Flow (DCF) Analysis:

The DCF method is a valuation method that estimates the future cash flows of a company and discounts them back to their present value using a discount rate. The DCF method is based on the idea that the value of a stock is equal to the present value of its expected future cash flows. The DCF method is widely used by investors to value stocks, but it requires a lot of assumptions about future growth rates, discount rates, and other factors.

Price-to-Earnings (P/E) Ratio:

The P/E ratio is a commonly used valuation method that compares a company's stock price to its earnings per share (EPS). The ratio is calculated by dividing the stock price by the EPS. A high P/E ratio suggests that investors are willing to pay more for the stock, indicating that the company is expected to grow or generate higher earnings in the future.

Price-to-Sales (P/S) Ratio:

The P/S ratio compares a company's stock price to its revenue per share. It is calculated by dividing the stock price by the revenue per share. This ratio is useful for valuing companies that have yet to turn a profit or have inconsistent earnings.

Price-to-Book (P/B) Ratio:

The P/B ratio compares a company's stock price to its book value per share, which is the value of a company's assets minus its liabilities divided by the number of outstanding shares. A low P/B ratio suggests that the company may be undervalued, while a high ratio suggests that the company may be overvalued.

Dividend Discount Model (DDM):

The DDM is a valuation method that estimates the value of a company's stock by forecasting its future dividends and discounting them back to their present value. The model assumes that the value of a company's stock is equal to the sum of its expected future dividends.

Comparable Analysis:

Comparable analysis involves comparing the financial metrics of a company to those of similar companies in the same industry. This method is often used to determine if a company is undervalued or overvalued relative to its peers.

Asset-Based Valuation:

This method estimates the value of a company's assets, including its tangible and intangible assets, and subtracts its liabilities. The resulting value represents the company's net asset value (NAV). This method is often used for companies with a significant amount of tangible assets, such as real estate or manufacturing companies.

In summary, there are various valuation methods and techniques that investors use to determine the fair value of a stock or a company's shares. Each method has its strengths and weaknesses, and investors often use a combination of methods to arrive at a more accurate valuation. Ultimately, the goal is to determine whether a stock is undervalued, fairly valued, or overvalued, and make an investment decision based on that determination.

### *Analyzing industry and market trends*

Analyzing industry and market trends is an important aspect of stock analysis. Understanding the current and future trends in an industry can provide valuable insight into the potential growth and profitability of a company. Here are some key factors to consider when analyzing industry and market trends for stock analysis:

Market Size and Growth:

The size and growth of a market can have a significant impact on a company's potential for growth and profitability. Look for trends in market size and growth rates to determine whether an industry is expanding or contracting.

Competitive Landscape:

Analyzing the competitive landscape can help you understand the market share and competitive advantage of a company within its industry. Look at the number and strength of competitors in the industry, as well as their market share, pricing strategies, and product offerings.

Regulatory Environment:

The regulatory environment can have a significant impact on a company's operations and profitability. Look for trends in regulation within the industry to determine the potential risks and opportunities for the company.

Technological Advancements:

Advancements in technology can create new opportunities and disrupt established industries. Look for trends in technological advancements within the industry to determine whether a company is well-positioned to take advantage of these opportunities or is at risk of being disrupted.

Consumer Behavior:

Consumer behavior can also have a significant impact on the potential growth and profitability of a company. Look for trends in consumer behavior within the industry, such as changing preferences or increasing demand for certain products or services.

Economic Conditions:

The overall economic conditions can also have an impact on the performance of companies within an industry. Look for trends in the economy, such as inflation rates, interest rates, and unemployment rates, to determine the potential risks and opportunities for the company.

Globalization:

Globalization can create new opportunities and challenges for companies operating in an industry. Look for trends in globalization, such as the growth of international trade and the increasing presence of global competitors, to determine the potential risks and opportunities for the company.

In summary, analyzing industry and market trends is an important aspect of stock analysis. By understanding the current and future trends within an industry, investors can gain valuable insight into the potential growth and profitability of a company. It is important to consider a range of factors, including market size and growth, competitive landscape, regulatory environment, technological advancements, consumer behavior, economic conditions, and globalization, to make informed investment decisions.

### Identifying and assessing risks

Identifying and assessing risks is an important part of stock analysis. Every investment comes with some level of risk, and it is important to identify and assess those risks before making an investment decision. Here are some key factors to consider when identifying and assessing risks for stocks:

Business Risk:

Business risk refers to the risks associated with a company's operations, such as competition, technological changes, supply chain disruptions, and changes in consumer preferences. Look for trends in the industry and competitive landscape to assess the potential risks and opportunities for a company.

Financial Risk:

Financial risk refers to the risks associated with a company's financial position, such as high debt levels, low profitability, and liquidity issues. Look at a company's financial statements to assess its financial health and identify any potential risks.

Market Risk:

Market risk refers to the risks associated with broader market conditions, such as economic downturns, geopolitical events, and changes in interest rates. Look for trends in the economy and broader market conditions to assess the potential risks and opportunities for a company.

Regulatory Risk:

Regulatory risk refers to the risks associated with changes in regulations or laws that could impact a company's operations or profitability. Look at the regulatory environment within the industry to assess the potential risks and opportunities for a company.

Environmental, Social, and Governance (ESG) Risk:

ESG risk refers to the risks associated with a company's impact on the environment, social issues, and governance practices. Look at a company's ESG policies and practices to assess its sustainability and potential risks and opportunities.

Reputation Risk:

Reputation risk refers to the risks associated with negative publicity or public perception of a company. Look at a company's history and current public perception to assess its reputation risk.

Operational Risk:

Operational risk refers to the risks associated with a company's internal processes, such as IT systems failures, supply chain disruptions, and human errors. Look at a company's operational processes and procedures to assess its operational risk.

In summary, identifying and assessing risks is an important aspect of stock analysis. It is important to consider a range of factors, including business risk, financial risk, market risk, regulatory risk, ESG risk, reputation risk, and operational risk, to make informed investment decisions. By understanding the potential risks and opportunities associated with a company, investors can make more informed decisions and manage their investment portfolios more effectively.

# Chapter 4: Strategies for Stock Investing

In this chapter we will cover the following topics:

- *Growth investing vs. value investing*
- *Income investing vs. capital gains investing*
- *Long-term vs. short-term investing*
- *Diversification and asset allocation*
- *Setting investment goals and developing a plan*

### Growth investing vs. value investing

Investing in the stock market can be a daunting task, especially when there are so many different investment strategies to choose from. Two popular approaches are growth investing and value investing. In this section, we will explore the key differences between these two investment strategies, their advantages and disadvantages, and how to decide which approach may be suitable for your investment goals.

### Growth Investing:

Growth investing is a strategy that focuses on investing in companies that are expected to grow at a faster rate than the overall market or their peers. These companies typically reinvest their earnings into expanding their businesses, developing new products or services, and entering new markets. Growth companies are often characterized by high revenue growth rates, high price-to-earnings ratios (P/E ratios), and low dividend yields.

*Advantages of Growth Investing:*

One of the main advantages of growth investing is the potential for high returns. Growth companies that are successful in expanding their businesses can experience exponential growth in their stock prices. For example, Amazon's stock price has grown over 1,000% in the past ten years due to its successful expansion into new markets and product offerings.

Another advantage of growth investing is the potential for capital gains. As growth companies reinvest their earnings into expanding their businesses, their stock prices may appreciate significantly, resulting in capital gains for investors.

*Disadvantages of Growth Investing:*

One disadvantage of growth investing is the potential for volatility. Growth companies may experience rapid price movements as their revenue and earnings growth rates fluctuate. This can result in large losses for investors if the company's growth slows down or if market sentiment turns negative.

Another disadvantage of growth investing is the high valuations of growth stocks. Growth companies with high revenue growth rates and low dividend yields often have high P/E ratios, which means that their stock prices are relatively expensive compared to their earnings. This can make it difficult to find undervalued growth companies to invest in.

**Value Investing:**

Value investing is a strategy that focuses on investing in companies that are undervalued by the market. These companies are often established, profitable companies that are trading at a discount to their intrinsic value. Value companies are often characterized by low P/E ratios, high dividend yields, and stable earnings growth rates.

*Advantages of Value Investing:*

One of the main advantages of value investing is the potential for steady returns. Value companies are often more stable and less volatile than growth companies, which can make them less risky investments. Value companies also tend to pay dividends, which provides investors with a steady stream of income.

Another advantage of value investing is the potential for capital gains. If a value company's stock price appreciates to reflect its intrinsic value, investors can realize significant capital gains.

*Disadvantages of Value Investing:*

One disadvantage of value investing is the potential for limited upside potential. Value companies may not experience the same level of growth as growth companies, which can limit the potential for significant capital gains.

Another disadvantage of value investing is the potential for value traps. Some companies may appear undervalued based on traditional valuation metrics, but their stock prices may remain depressed for extended periods due to fundamental weaknesses in the company's business model or industry.

**How to Decide between Growth Investing and Value Investing:**

Deciding between growth investing and value investing ultimately depends on your investment goals, risk tolerance, and investment timeframe. Growth investing may be suitable for investors who are willing to take on more risk in exchange for the potential for high returns, while value investing may be suitable for investors who prefer more stable, less volatile investments with a steady stream of income.

It is important to note that there is no one-size-fits-all investment strategy, and investors should consider their own investment objectives, financial situation, and risk tolerance before making any investment decisions.

*Income investing vs. capital gains investing*

When it comes to investing in the stock market, there are different strategies you can employ depending on your investment goals. Two popular approaches are income investing and capital gains investing. In this section, we will explore the key differences between these two investment strategies, their advantages and disadvantages, and how to decide which approach may be suitable for your investment goals.

**Income Investing:**

Income investing is a strategy that focuses on investing in stocks that pay regular dividends. Dividends are a portion of a company's profits that are distributed to shareholders. Income investors seek out stocks with high dividend yields, which is the dividend payment expressed as a percentage of the stock price.

*Advantages of Income Investing:*

One of the main advantages of income investing is the potential for a steady stream of income. Dividend-paying stocks provide investors with a regular source of income, which can be especially beneficial for retirees or investors who rely on their investments for income.

Another advantage of income investing is the potential for lower risk. Companies that pay dividends are often more established and stable, which can make them less volatile and less risky than growth companies.

*Disadvantages of Income Investing:*

One disadvantage of income investing is the potential for lower capital gains. Dividend-paying stocks may not appreciate as quickly as growth stocks, which can limit the potential for significant capital gains.

Another disadvantage of income investing is the potential for dividend cuts. Companies can reduce or eliminate their dividends at any time, which can result in lower income for investors and a decline in the stock price.

**Capital Gains Investing:**

Capital gains investing is a strategy that focuses on investing in stocks that have the potential for significant price appreciation. Capital gains investors seek out stocks with strong growth potential, which can be fueled by factors such as increasing revenue, expanding profit margins, or entering new markets.

*Advantages of Capital Gains Investing:*

One of the main advantages of capital gains investing is the potential for significant price appreciation. Stocks with strong growth potential can experience rapid price increases, which can result in significant capital gains for investors.

Another advantage of capital gains investing is the potential for diversification. Growth stocks can come from a variety of industries, which can help investors diversify their portfolios and reduce risk.

*Disadvantages of Capital Gains Investing:*

One disadvantage of capital gains investing is the potential for higher risk. Growth companies are often riskier than established, dividend-paying companies because they may be in the early stages of growth and have less established business models.

Another disadvantage of capital gains investing is the potential for volatility. Growth companies may experience rapid price movements as their revenue and earnings growth rates fluctuate. This can result in large losses for investors if the company's growth slows down or if market sentiment turns negative.

**How to Decide between Income Investing and Capital Gains Investing:**

Deciding between income investing and capital gains investing ultimately depends on your investment goals, risk tolerance, and investment timeframe. Income investing may be suitable for investors who are looking for a steady stream of income and are willing to accept lower potential capital gains. Capital gains investing may be suitable for investors who are willing to take on more risk in exchange for the potential for significant capital gains.

It is important to note that there is no one-size-fits-all investment strategy, and investors should consider their own investment objectives, financial situation, and risk tolerance before making any investment decisions. A balanced approach that combines both income and capital gains investing strategies may be appropriate for some investors.

*Long-term vs. short-term investing*

When it comes to investing in the stock market, there are different strategies you can employ depending on your investment goals. Two popular approaches are long-term investing and short-term investing. In this section, we will explore the key differences between these two investment strategies, their advantages and disadvantages, and how to decide which approach may be suitable for your investment goals.

**Long-Term Investing:**

Long-term investing is a strategy that focuses on holding stocks for an extended period, typically several years or more. Long-term investors look for companies with strong fundamentals, such as solid financials, a competitive advantage, and a history of consistent growth. They seek to capture the long-term growth potential of these companies, rather than making short-term trades based on market fluctuations.

*Advantages of Long-Term Investing:*

One of the main advantages of long-term investing is the potential for higher returns. Over the long term, stocks have historically provided higher returns than other asset classes such as bonds or cash. By holding stocks for an extended period, long-term investors may be able to capture the full growth potential of the companies in which they invest.

Another advantage of long-term investing is the potential for lower taxes. Long-term capital gains taxes are generally lower than short-term capital gains taxes, which can help investors keep more of their gains.

*Disadvantages of Long-Term Investing:*

One disadvantage of long-term investing is the potential for lower liquidity. Stocks can be difficult to sell quickly, especially during market downturns, which can make it challenging for investors to access their funds when they need them.

Another disadvantage of long-term investing is the potential for missing out on short-term gains. Long-term investors may miss out on opportunities to profit from short-term market fluctuations or to capitalize on short-term news events.

**Short-Term Investing:**

Short-term investing is a strategy that focuses on making trades based on short-term market fluctuations or news events. Short-term investors seek to profit from these movements by buying and selling stocks quickly, often within days or weeks.

*Advantages of Short-Term Investing:*

One advantage of short-term investing is the potential for quick profits. Short-term traders can capitalize on short-term market movements and news events, potentially generating significant returns in a short period.

Another advantage of short-term investing is the potential for higher liquidity. Short-term traders can quickly buy and sell stocks, which can make it easier for them to access their funds when they need them.

*Disadvantages of Short-Term Investing:*

One disadvantage of short-term investing is the potential for higher taxes. Short-term capital gains taxes are generally higher than long-term capital gains taxes, which can eat into investors' profits.

Another disadvantage of short-term investing is the potential for higher risk. Short-term traders may be more exposed to market volatility and news events, which can result in large losses if the market turns against them.

**How to Decide between Long-Term Investing and Short-Term Investing:**

Deciding between long-term investing and short-term investing ultimately depends on your investment goals, risk tolerance, and investment timeframe. Long-term investing may be suitable for investors who are looking for stable, long-term growth and are willing to accept lower liquidity and potentially miss out on short-term gains. Short-term investing may be suitable for investors who are comfortable with higher risk and are looking for quick profits.

It is important to note that there is no one-size-fits-all investment strategy, and investors should consider their own investment objectives, financial situation, and risk tolerance before making any investment decisions. A balanced approach that combines both long-term and short-term investing strategies may be appropriate for some investors.

*Diversification and asset allocation*

Diversification and asset allocation are two key concepts that are essential for any investor looking to build a successful stock portfolio. In this section, we will explore what diversification and asset allocation are, why they are important, and how to implement them effectively.

**Diversification:**

Diversification is the strategy of investing in a variety of different stocks to spread out risk and reduce the impact of market volatility on your portfolio. Diversification involves investing in stocks from different industries, sectors, and geographies to minimize the risk of losses due to the poor performance of a single stock or sector.

*Advantages of Diversification:*

One of the main advantages of diversification is that it helps to reduce risk. By investing in a range of different stocks, you spread out the risk of your portfolio and minimize the impact of market volatility on your returns.

Another advantage of diversification is that it can help to maximize returns. By investing in a range of different stocks, you have the potential to capture returns from different sectors and industries, which can help to improve the overall performance of your portfolio.

*Disadvantages of Diversification:*

One disadvantage of diversification is that it can limit potential gains. When you invest in a diversified portfolio, you may miss out on the opportunity to achieve significant gains from a single stock that performs exceptionally well.

Another disadvantage of diversification is that it can increase complexity. Managing a diversified portfolio can be challenging, especially if you are investing in a large number of stocks.

**Asset Allocation:**

Asset allocation is the strategy of dividing your portfolio into different asset classes, such as stocks, bonds, and cash, to achieve a specific investment objective. Asset allocation involves determining the right mix of asset classes for your portfolio based on your investment goals, risk tolerance, and time horizon.

*Advantages of Asset Allocation:*

One of the main advantages of asset allocation is that it helps to minimize risk. By investing in a range of different asset classes, you spread out the risk of your portfolio and minimize the impact of market volatility on your returns.

Another advantage of asset allocation is that it can help to maximize returns. By investing in a range of different asset classes, you have the potential to capture returns from different sectors and industries, which can help to improve the overall performance of your portfolio.

*Disadvantages of Asset Allocation:*

One disadvantage of asset allocation is that it can limit potential gains. When you invest in a diversified portfolio, you may miss out on the opportunity to achieve significant gains from a single stock that performs exceptionally well.

Another disadvantage of asset allocation is that it can be difficult to determine the right mix of asset classes for your portfolio. The optimal mix of asset classes will depend on your investment goals, risk tolerance, and time horizon, which can be challenging to determine.

**Implementing Diversification and Asset Allocation:**

To implement diversification and asset allocation effectively, you should start by determining your investment goals, risk tolerance, and time horizon. You should then create a diversified portfolio that includes stocks from different sectors and industries, as well as bonds and other asset classes as appropriate for your investment objectives. You should also regularly review and rebalance your portfolio to ensure that it continues to meet your investment goals and risk tolerance.

In conclusion, diversification and asset allocation are two key concepts that are essential for any investor looking to build a successful stock portfolio. By investing in a diversified portfolio that includes a range of different stocks and asset classes, you can minimize risk and maximize returns, while also achieving your investment goals and objectives.

### Setting investment goals and developing a plan

Setting investment goals and developing a plan for stock investing is a critical step towards building a successful portfolio. In this section, we will explore the importance of setting investment goals, how to develop a plan for stock investing, and some best practices for achieving your investment objectives.

**Setting Investment Goals:**

Before investing in stocks, it's essential to define your investment goals. Your investment goals will determine the type of stocks you should invest in, the amount of risk you should take, and the timeline for your investments. Some common investment goals include:

*Wealth Accumulation:* This goal involves building wealth over the long term and may involve a buy-and-hold strategy.

*Income Generation:* This goal involves generating income from dividends and interest and may involve investing in high dividend-paying stocks.

*Capital Preservation:* This goal involves minimizing risk and preserving capital and may involve investing in low-risk stocks or fixed-income securities.

*Speculation:* This goal involves taking high-risk investments in the hopes of generating high returns and may involve investing in emerging markets or start-up companies.

**Developing a Plan for Stock Investing:**

Once you've defined your investment goals, you can develop a plan for stock investing. Your plan should include the following elements:

*Asset Allocation:* Determine the percentage of your portfolio that you will allocate to stocks based on your investment goals and risk tolerance.

*Stock Selection:* Identify the types of stocks that align with your investment goals and select individual stocks or exchange-traded funds (ETFs) that fit your criteria.

*Diversification:* Ensure that your portfolio is diversified across different sectors and industries to minimize risk.

*Risk Management:* Establish risk management strategies, such as stop-loss orders or position sizing, to protect your portfolio against significant losses.

**Best Practices for Achieving Your Investment Objectives:**

To achieve your investment objectives, it's essential to follow some best practices, including:

*Monitor Your Portfolio:* Regularly review your portfolio to ensure that it's aligned with your investment goals and risk tolerance.

*Rebalance Your Portfolio:* Adjust your portfolio as needed to maintain the desired asset allocation and diversification.

*Invest for the Long Term:* Stock investing is a long-term strategy, and it's essential to stay invested and avoid reacting to short-term market fluctuations.

*Stay Informed:* Stay up-to-date on market trends and news that could impact your investments and be prepared to adjust your strategy accordingly.

In conclusion, setting investment goals and developing a plan for stock investing is a critical step towards building a successful portfolio. By defining your investment goals, developing a plan that aligns with your goals and risk tolerance, and following best practices for achieving your objectives, you can increase your chances of building wealth and achieving financial independence over the long term.

In this chapter we will cover the following topics:

- *Choosing a broker and opening an account*
- *Placing orders and executing trades*
- *Types of orders and their advantages and disadvantages*
- *Timing your trades and managing your portfolio*

### Choosing a broker and opening an account

When it comes to investing in the stock market, one of the first steps you'll need to take is to choose a broker and open a trading account. A broker is an individual or firm that acts as an intermediary between buyers and sellers of financial securities, such as stocks, bonds, and mutual funds. They help facilitate the buying and selling of securities and often provide additional services such as research and education to their clients. Here are some steps to help you choose a broker and open an account:

*Step 1: Determine Your Investment Needs*

Before choosing a broker, it's important to determine your investment needs. Do you want to invest in individual stocks or do you prefer to invest in mutual funds or exchange-traded funds (ETFs)? Do you have a specific investment strategy or risk tolerance? Understanding your investment needs can help you choose a broker that aligns with your goals.

*Step 2: Research Potential Brokers*

Once you have a clear understanding of your investment needs, it's time to research potential brokers. Consider factors such as fees, investment options, trading platforms, customer service, and reputation. Look for online reviews and ratings, as well as recommendations from friends and family.

*Step 3: Compare Fees and Commissions*

When comparing brokers, be sure to look at their fee structure. Some brokers charge a commission per trade, while others charge a flat fee per trade. Additionally, some brokers may charge annual account fees or other miscellaneous fees. Be sure to compare the total cost of trading with each broker to ensure you're getting the best deal.

*Step 4: Check Investment Options*

Make sure the broker you choose offers the investment options you're interested in. For example, if you're interested in investing in mutual funds, make sure the broker offers a wide selection of funds with low expense ratios. If you're interested in individual stocks, make sure the broker offers access to the exchanges and markets you're interested in.

*Step 5: Open an Account*

Once you've chosen a broker, the next step is to open an account. This typically involves filling out an online application, providing some personal information, and agreeing to the broker's terms and conditions. You may also be required to provide proof of identity and income, such as a driver's license and a recent pay stub.

*Step 6: Fund Your Account*

After your account is open, you'll need to fund it with cash or securities. Some brokers may require a minimum deposit to open an account, so be sure to check their requirements before opening an account. Once your account is funded, you can start trading.

In conclusion, choosing a broker and opening an account is an important step in investing in the stock market. By following these steps, you can find a broker that meets your investment needs and start building your investment portfolio.


### Placing orders and executing trades

After you've opened a trading account with a broker, the next step is to place orders and execute trades. This process involves buying and selling stocks or other securities in the market. Here are the steps to place orders and execute trades:

*Step 1: Choose the Security to Trade*

The first step in placing an order is to choose the security you want to trade. This could be a stock, ETF, mutual fund, or any other security that's available in the market. Before placing an order, it's important to do your research and analyze the security to determine whether it's a good investment opportunity.

*Step 2: Choose the Type of Order*

Once you've selected the security you want to trade, the next step is to choose the type of order you want to place. There are several types of orders you can place, including market orders, limit orders, stop orders, and more. Each type of order has its own unique characteristics and benefits, so it's important to understand the differences between them before placing an order.

*Step 3: Set the Price and Quantity*

After choosing the type of order, the next step is to set the price and quantity of the trade. For a market order, you simply enter the number of shares you want to buy or sell, and the broker will execute the trade at the current market price. For a limit order, you set a specific price at which you want to buy or sell the security. The trade will only be executed if the security reaches your specified price.

*Step 4: Submit the Order*

After setting the price and quantity, the next step is to submit the order to the broker. This is typically done through the broker's trading platform, which may be accessed through a web browser, mobile app, or desktop application. Once the order is submitted, it's routed to the market for execution.

*Step 5: Monitor the Trade*

After the order is submitted, it's important to monitor the trade to ensure it's executed properly. This may involve tracking the price of the security and making adjustments to the order if necessary. It's also important to keep an eye on any news or market events that could affect the price of the security.

*Step 6: Review the Trade Confirmation*

Once the trade is executed, the broker will provide a trade confirmation that includes details such as the price, quantity, and execution time of the trade. It's important to review this confirmation carefully to ensure that the trade was executed as intended.

In conclusion, placing orders and executing trades is an important part of investing in the stock market. By following these steps and choosing the right type of order, you can ensure that your trades are executed properly and that you're getting the best possible price for your investments.

### Types of orders and their advantages and disadvantages

When it comes to trading stocks, there are several different types of orders that investors can use to buy and sell securities. Each type of order has its own advantages and disadvantages, and it's important to understand the differences between them before placing an order. Here are some of the most common types of stock orders and their pros and cons:

*Market Orders*

Market orders are the most basic type of order and are executed at the current market price. When you place a market order, you're essentially telling your broker to buy or sell the security immediately, regardless of the current price. The main advantage of a market order is that it's fast and easy to execute. The main disadvantage is that you may not get the best possible price, especially if the market is volatile or there's low liquidity.

*Limit Orders*

Limit orders allow you to set a specific price at which you're willing to buy or sell a security. For example, if you want to buy a stock at a certain price or lower, you would place a buy limit order. If the stock reaches that price or lower, the order will be executed. The main advantage of a limit order is that it allows you to control the price at which you buy or sell a security. The main disadvantage is that the order may not be executed if the security doesn't reach your specified price.

*Stop Orders*

Stop orders are used to limit losses or protect profits. There are two types of stop orders: stop-loss orders and stop-limit orders. A stop-loss order is an order to sell a security if it falls to a certain price or lower. The idea is to limit potential losses if the security drops in price. A stop-limit order is a combination of a limit order and a stop order. With a stop-limit order, you set a stop price and a limit price. If the security falls to the stop price, the order becomes a limit order to sell at the limit price or better. The main advantage of a stop order is that it can help protect your portfolio from significant losses. The main disadvantage is that it may be triggered by short-term market fluctuations, which could result in selling a security at a lower price than you intended.

*Trailing Stop Orders*

Trailing stop orders are similar to stop-loss orders, but they allow you to set a trailing price that adjusts with the market price. For example, if you set a trailing stop order at 10% below the market price, and the market price rises, the trailing stop will adjust to reflect the new market price. If the market price falls by more than 10%, the order will be triggered. The main advantage of a trailing stop order is that it allows you to lock in profits while still allowing for potential gains. The main disadvantage is that it may not be effective in a volatile market.

*All-or-None Orders*

All-or-none orders are orders that require the entire order to be executed at once, or not at all. The main advantage of an all-or-none order is that it ensures that you'll receive the entire quantity of shares you're looking to buy or sell. The main disadvantage is that it may be difficult to execute in a volatile market, and may result in missed opportunities.

In conclusion, there are several different types of stock orders that investors can use to buy and sell securities. Each type of order has its own advantages and disadvantages, and it's important to understand the differences between them before placing an order. By choosing the right type of order for your investment strategy, you can help ensure that your trades are executed properly and that you're getting the best possible price for your investments.


**Timing your trades and managing your portfolio**

Timing your trades and managing your portfolio are critical aspects of successful stock investing. Here are some key considerations to keep in mind:

*Market Timing*

Market timing refers to the practice of buying and selling securities based on predictions of market trends. While some investors believe that they can predict market movements and time their trades accordingly, most experts agree that it's extremely difficult to consistently time the market. Attempting to time the market can lead to missed opportunities and increased risk, as you may end up buying high and selling low. Instead of trying to time the market, it's generally better to focus on building a diversified portfolio of high-quality stocks that you're comfortable holding for the long term.

*Asset Allocation*

Asset allocation is the practice of dividing your investment portfolio among different asset classes, such as stocks, bonds, and cash. The goal of asset allocation is to balance risk and reward based on your investment goals and risk tolerance. Generally speaking, younger investors with a longer time horizon can afford to take more risk and may want to allocate a larger portion of their portfolio to stocks. Older investors who are closer to retirement may want to focus more on preserving capital and may allocate a larger portion of their portfolio to bonds and cash.

*Rebalancing*

Rebalancing involves periodically adjusting your portfolio to maintain your desired asset allocation. For example, if your target allocation for stocks is 60%, but your stock holdings have increased in value to 70% of your portfolio, you may need to sell some stocks and buy more bonds or cash to bring your portfolio back into balance. Rebalancing can help you manage risk and maintain your long-term investment strategy.

*Risk Management*

Risk management is the practice of identifying and managing potential risks to your portfolio. Some key strategies for managing risk include diversification, using stop-loss orders, and setting realistic investment goals. It's also important to stay informed about economic and market developments that could impact your portfolio.

*Tax Management*

Tax management is the practice of managing your portfolio in a tax-efficient manner. Some key strategies for tax management include holding investments in tax-advantaged accounts, such as IRAs and 401(k)s, and being mindful of tax consequences when buying and selling securities. It's also important to consider the impact of taxes on your investment returns and to work with a tax professional to develop a tax-efficient investment strategy.

In conclusion, timing your trades and managing your portfolio are critical aspects of successful stock investing. By focusing on asset allocation, rebalancing, risk management, and tax management, you can build a diversified portfolio that's well-positioned to achieve your long-term investment goals. It's also important to avoid trying to time the market and to stay focused on your investment strategy, even during periods of market volatility.

# Chapter 6: Advanced Stock Investing Techniques

In this chapter we will cover the following topics:

- *Technical analysis and charting*
- *Options trading and hedging strategies*
- *Leveraging and margin trading*
- *Investing in IPOs and other emerging opportunities*

### Technical analysis and charting

Technical analysis is a method used in stock investing that focuses on analyzing historical market data, such as price and volume, to identify patterns and trends that may indicate future price movements. Charting is a key component of technical analysis and involves using graphical representations of price and volume data to identify patterns and trends.

Charts are used to display the movement of a stock's price over time. There are many types of charts, but the most common ones used in technical analysis are line charts, bar charts, and candlestick charts. Line charts are the simplest type of chart and display the closing price of a stock for each day in a single line. Bar charts show the opening, closing, high, and low prices for each day in a vertical bar. Candlestick charts are similar to bar charts but use colored candles to indicate price movements.

Technical analysts use charts to identify patterns and trends in a stock's price movement. For example, they may look for support and resistance levels, which are levels at which the price of a stock has historically had difficulty breaking through. Technical analysts also look for chart patterns, such as triangles, flags, and head and shoulders formations, which can signal future price movements.

In addition to charting, technical analysis also involves the use of technical indicators. Technical indicators are mathematical calculations based on price and volume data that are used to help predict future price movements. Some commonly used technical indicators include moving averages, relative strength index (RSI), and stochastic oscillator. The RSI ranges from 0 to 100 and is considered overbought when it is above 70 and oversold when it is below 30.

Moving averages are used to smooth out price fluctuations and show the average price of a stock over a specified time period. The RSI is used to measure the strength of a stock's price movement and identify overbought or oversold conditions. The stochastic oscillator is used to identify potential reversals in a stock's price movement.

While technical analysis and charting can be valuable tools for stock investing, it is important to remember that they are not foolproof. Market sentiment can change quickly, and no indicator or chart pattern can predict the future with 100% accuracy. As with any investment strategy, it is important to do your research and use technical analysis and charting in conjunction with other methods of analysis, such as fundamental analysis and market research.

### Options trading and hedging strategies

Options trading is a popular strategy used by investors to manage risk and potentially increase profits. Options are contracts that give investors the right, but not the obligation, to buy or sell an underlying asset at a specific price and time. In the context of stock investing, options contracts allow investors to buy or sell shares of a stock at a predetermined price, known as the strike price.

There are two main types of options contracts: call options and put options. A call option gives the holder the right to buy an underlying asset at a specific price and time, while a put option gives the holder the right to sell an underlying asset at a specific price and time.

Options trading can be used for a variety of purposes, including speculation and hedging. Speculators use options trading to try to profit from the price movements of a stock, while hedgers use options trading to protect their portfolio from potential losses.

One popular hedging strategy is the use of protective puts. A protective put involves buying a put option for a stock that an investor already owns. If the price of the stock drops, the investor can exercise the put option and sell the stock at the strike price, which helps to limit their losses.

Another hedging strategy is the use of covered calls. A covered call involves selling a call option for a stock that an investor already owns. If the price of the stock does not reach the strike price, the investor keeps the premium from the sale of the call option. If the price of the stock does reach the strike price, the investor must sell the stock at the predetermined price, which helps to limit their losses.

Options trading can be complex and carries significant risk. It is important for investors to thoroughly understand the mechanics of options trading before engaging in it. In addition, investors should always use options trading in conjunction with other investment strategies and risk management techniques, such as diversification and asset allocation.

Overall, options trading and hedging strategies can be valuable tools for investors looking to manage risk and potentially increase profits. However, it is important for investors to understand the risks and limitations of options trading before using it as part of their investment strategy.

### Leveraging and margin trading

Leveraging and margin trading are advanced investment strategies that involve borrowing funds to invest in the stock market. These strategies can be very risky, but they can also provide investors with the potential for higher returns.

Leveraging is the use of borrowed funds to increase the potential returns of an investment. This can be done through a variety of methods, such as buying stocks on margin, using options contracts, or investing in leveraged exchange-traded funds (ETFs).

Margin trading is a type of leveraging that involves borrowing funds from a broker to buy stocks. When an investor buys stocks on margin, they put up a portion of the purchase price, called the margin, and borrow the rest of the funds from their broker. This allows investors to buy more stocks than they would be able to with their own funds, increasing their potential returns.

However, margin trading also carries significant risk. If the value of the stocks purchased on margin declines, the investor may be required to deposit additional funds to cover the margin, or their broker may sell their stocks to cover the loss. This can result in significant losses for the investor.

Leveraged ETFs are another type of leveraging strategy that involves investing in ETFs that use borrowed funds to amplify their returns. While leveraged ETFs can provide higher returns, they also carry higher risk, as the use of borrowed funds can amplify losses as well as gains.

Overall, leveraging and margin trading can be risky investment strategies and should only be used by experienced investors who understand the potential risks and limitations. It is important to carefully consider the risks and potential returns before engaging in these strategies, and to use them in conjunction with other investment strategies and risk management techniques, such as diversification and asset allocation.

### Investing in IPOs and other emerging opportunities

Investing in IPOs and other emerging opportunities can provide investors with the potential for significant returns, but also carries significant risk. IPOs, or initial public offerings, are when a company first issues shares of stock to the public. These stocks can be very attractive to investors, as they often offer the potential for rapid growth and significant returns.

However, investing in IPOs can also be very risky, as newly public companies may be untested in the public markets and may not have a proven track record of success. In addition, the initial offering price of an IPO can be inflated, leading to a decline in the stock price after the initial hype wears off.

Other emerging opportunities in the stock market may include investing in companies in emerging industries or investing in stocks that are not yet widely known or followed by the market. While these opportunities can provide investors with the potential for significant returns, they also carry significant risk, as these companies may be untested or may face significant competition in their industry.

To mitigate risk when investing in IPOs and other emerging opportunities, it is important for investors to conduct thorough research and analysis of the company and its industry. This may include reviewing the company's financial statements, analyzing its competitors, and assessing the potential for future growth.

In addition, it is important for investors to maintain a diversified portfolio that includes a mix of stocks in different industries and market sectors. This can help to mitigate risk by spreading investments across multiple areas of the market.

Overall, investing in IPOs and other emerging opportunities can provide investors with the potential for significant returns, but also carries significant risk. It is important for investors to carefully consider the risks and potential returns before engaging in these strategies and to use them in conjunction with other investment strategies and risk management techniques, such as diversification and asset allocation.

# Chapter 7: Risks and Challenges of Stock Investing

In this chapter we will cover the following topics:

- *Market volatility and fluctuations*
- *Company-specific risks and controversies*
- *Economic and political risks and uncertainties*
- *Behavioral biases and emotional pitfalls*
- *Managing risks and minimizing losses*

## Market volatility and fluctuations

Market volatility and fluctuations are inevitable parts of stock investing. The stock market is constantly moving up and down, and it can be challenging for investors to navigate these changes. Understanding the relationship between market volatility, risk, and challenges in stock investing is crucial for any investor looking to succeed in the stock market.

Market volatility refers to the degree of variation of stock prices over time. When the market experiences high volatility, stock prices can fluctuate rapidly and significantly. These fluctuations can be caused by a variety of factors, including economic indicators, geopolitical events, and company-specific news. Volatility can be measured using different metrics, such as standard deviation, beta, or the VIX (volatility index).

While market volatility can provide opportunities for investors to make profits, it also introduces risks and challenges. One of the main risks of investing in volatile markets is the potential for significant losses. When stock prices fall rapidly, investors may panic and sell their shares, leading to even greater declines. This phenomenon is known as a "market crash." Additionally, high volatility can make it difficult for investors to make informed decisions, as stock prices can fluctuate so rapidly that it's hard to know whether a particular investment is a good buy or sell.

Another challenge that investors face in volatile markets is increased uncertainty. When the market is stable, investors can rely on past performance to make informed decisions. However, in volatile markets, past performance may not be a reliable indicator of future performance. This uncertainty can make it difficult for investors to predict how their investments will perform, leading to increased risk.

Despite these challenges, there are strategies that investors can use to manage risk and succeed in volatile markets. One approach is diversification, which involves investing in a variety of different stocks and asset classes. Diversification can help reduce the impact of volatility on an investor's portfolio by spreading risk across multiple investments.

Another strategy is to invest for the long term. While short-term volatility can be unsettling, over the long term, stock prices tend to rise. By investing for the long term, investors can ride out short-term volatility and potentially benefit from long-term growth.

In conclusion, market volatility and fluctuations are a fact of life in stock investing. While they introduce risks and challenges, they also provide opportunities for investors to make profits. By understanding the relationship between volatility, risk, and challenges, investors can develop strategies to manage risk and succeed in the stock market.

### Company-specific risks and controversies

When it comes to investing in the stock market, company-specific risks and controversies can present significant challenges and risks for investors. These risks can range from financial performance to ethical issues and can have a major impact on a company's stock price.

One of the most significant company-specific risks is financial performance. If a company's earnings or revenue growth do not meet expectations, investors may become concerned about the company's ability to generate profits and grow. This can lead to a decrease in stock price as investors sell off their shares.

Another company-specific risk is related to industry competition. If a company operates in a highly competitive industry, it may struggle to differentiate itself from its competitors, which can lead to decreased market share and profits. This risk is particularly relevant in industries with low barriers to entry, where new competitors can quickly enter the market and disrupt established players.

Ethical issues and controversies can also have a major impact on a company's stock price. Examples of such controversies include environmental disasters, labor violations, and product recalls. These controversies can result in negative media coverage, consumer backlash, and legal action, which can lead to decreased sales and profits. Additionally, ethical issues can damage a company's reputation, which can impact its ability to attract customers, employees, and investors.

Another company-specific risk is related to management decisions. Poor management decisions, such as excessive debt, mismanagement of resources, or ill-timed acquisitions, can result in significant losses for investors. Additionally, if a company's leadership team is perceived as being ineffective or unethical, this can lead to decreased investor confidence and a decline in stock price.

Despite these risks and challenges, there are strategies that investors can use to manage company-specific risks. One approach is to conduct thorough research and due diligence before investing in a company. This can involve analyzing a company's financial statements, assessing its competitive position, and investigating any potential ethical concerns. Additionally, diversification can help reduce the impact of individual company risks on an investor's portfolio by spreading risk across multiple investments.

In conclusion, company-specific risks and controversies can pose significant challenges and risks for investors. Understanding these risks and developing strategies to manage them is crucial for any investor looking to succeed in the stock market. By conducting thorough research and diversifying their portfolio, investors can potentially minimize the impact of company-specific risks on their investments.

### Economic and political risks and uncertainties

Investing in the stock market is inherently risky, and economic and political risks and uncertainties can add additional challenges for investors. These risks can range from inflation and interest rates to geopolitical tensions and trade disputes and can have a significant impact on the stock market.

One of the primary economic risks for investors is inflation. Inflation occurs when the general price level of goods and services increases, which can reduce the purchasing power of money. This can lead to decreased consumer spending, lower corporate profits, and a decline in the stock market. Additionally, rising interest rates can impact the stock market by increasing borrowing costs for companies and reducing consumer spending.

Geopolitical tensions and trade disputes can also pose significant risks for investors. If two or more countries are engaged in a trade dispute, this can lead to tariffs and other trade barriers, which can impact the profitability of companies that rely on international trade. Additionally, geopolitical tensions can lead to uncertainty and volatility in the stock market, as investors become nervous about the potential for conflict or instability.

Political risks and uncertainties can also impact the stock market. Elections, changes in government policies, and regulatory changes can all have a significant impact on the stock market. For example, if a new government comes into power and implements policies that are unfavorable to certain industries or companies, this can lead to a decline in their stock prices.

Despite these risks and challenges, there are strategies that investors can use to manage economic and political risks. One approach is to diversify their portfolio across different industries and asset classes. This can help reduce the impact of individual economic or political risks on an investor's overall portfolio.

Additionally, investors can stay informed about economic and political developments by following the news and analyzing economic data. This can help investors anticipate potential risks and make informed investment decisions.

In conclusion, economic and political risks and uncertainties can pose significant challenges and risks for investors. Understanding these risks and developing strategies to manage them is crucial for any investor looking to succeed in the stock market. By diversifying their portfolio and staying informed about economic and political developments, investors can potentially reduce the impact of these risks on their investments.

### Behavioral biases and emotional pitfalls

Behavioral biases and emotional pitfalls can have a significant impact on investment decisions and can lead to poor investment outcomes. As such, understanding these biases and pitfalls is crucial for any investor looking to succeed in the stock market.

One common behavioral bias is herd mentality. This bias refers to the tendency for individuals to follow the actions and beliefs of the crowd, even if those actions and beliefs may not be rational or based on sound evidence. In the context of the stock market, this can lead to a bubble, where investors become overly optimistic and bid up the prices of stocks to unsustainable levels.

Another common behavioral bias is overconfidence. This bias refers to the tendency for individuals to overestimate their own abilities and underestimate the probability of negative outcomes. In the context of the stock market, this can lead investors to take excessive risks, leading to significant losses.

*Fear and greed* are also common emotional pitfalls that can impact investment decisions. Fear can lead investors to panic and sell their investments during times of market volatility, potentially realizing significant losses. Conversely, greed can lead investors to become overly optimistic and take excessive risks, potentially leading to significant losses.

*Confirmation bias* is another behavioral bias that can impact investment decisions. This bias refers to the tendency for individuals to seek out information that confirms their existing beliefs and to ignore information that contradicts those beliefs. In the context of the stock market, this can lead investors to overvalue certain stocks and ignore warning signs that suggest those stocks may be overvalued.

To manage these behavioral biases and emotional pitfalls, investors can take a number of steps. One approach is to develop a disciplined investment strategy and stick to it, regardless of short-term market fluctuations. This can help investors avoid the pitfalls of herd mentality and overconfidence.

Another approach is to seek out diverse perspectives and challenge existing beliefs. This can help investors avoid confirmation bias and make more informed investment decisions. Additionally, investors can seek out the advice of financial professionals, who can provide guidance and expertise on managing behavioral biases and emotional pitfalls.

In conclusion, behavioral biases and emotional pitfalls can have a significant impact on investment decisions and can lead to poor investment outcomes. Understanding these biases and pitfalls is crucial for any investor looking to succeed in the stock market. By developing a disciplined investment strategy, seeking out diverse perspectives, and seeking the advice of financial professionals, investors can potentially avoid these biases and pitfalls and make more informed investment decisions.

### Managing risks and minimizing losses

Managing risks and minimizing losses is an essential aspect of successful stock investing. No investment is entirely risk-free, but there are strategies that investors can use to mitigate risk and reduce potential losses.

One approach to managing risk is to diversify a portfolio. Diversification involves spreading investments across different stocks, sectors, and asset classes to reduce the impact of any one investment on the overall portfolio. By diversifying a portfolio, investors can potentially reduce the impact of company-specific risks and market volatility.

Another approach is to use stop-loss orders. A stop-loss order is an order placed with a broker to sell a stock if it falls to a certain price. This can help investors limit their losses in the event of a significant market downturn or unexpected company-specific event.

Additionally, investors can use dollar-cost averaging to manage risk. Dollar-cost averaging involves investing a fixed amount of money at regular intervals, regardless of market conditions. This can help investors avoid the pitfalls of trying to time the market and potentially reduce the impact of short-term market fluctuations on their investments.

Investors can also use fundamental analysis to identify companies with strong financials and a competitive advantage. By investing in companies with a strong track record of financial performance, investors may be able to reduce the impact of company-specific risks and potentially achieve better long-term returns.

Finally, investors can stay informed about market developments and economic indicators to anticipate potential risks and make informed investment decisions. This can involve following financial news and analysis, monitoring economic data, and seeking out the advice of financial professionals.

In conclusion, managing risks and minimizing losses is a crucial aspect of successful stock investing. By diversifying a portfolio, using stop-loss orders, practicing dollar-cost averaging, using fundamental analysis, and staying informed about market developments, investors can potentially reduce risk and achieve better long-term returns. While no investment is entirely risk-free, these strategies can help investors navigate the challenges of stock investing and achieve their investment goals.

# Chapter 8: Conclusion and Resources

In this chapter we will cover the following topics:

- *Recap of key concepts and strategies*
- *Additional resources for stock investing*
- *FAQs and common misconceptions*
- *Next steps and recommended reading*

### Recap of key concepts and strategies

*Key concepts on investing in stocks:*

- ➤ Stocks are ownership stakes in a company, and their value can rise or fall based on the performance of the company and the overall market.
- ➤ Diversification is a key strategy for reducing risk. By investing in a variety of stocks across different industries and sectors, you can minimize the impact of any one stock or sector on your portfolio.
- ➤ Fundamental analysis involves examining a company's financial statements, management team, industry trends, and other factors to determine its value and growth potential.
- ➤ Technical analysis involves studying charts and other market data to identify trends and patterns that can help predict future stock prices.
- ➤ Dollar-cost averaging involves investing a fixed amount of money at regular intervals over time, which can help smooth out the impact of market volatility.
- ➤ Buy-and-hold investing involves holding onto stocks for the long term, rather than trying to time the market or make quick profits through frequent trading.
- ➤ Index funds are a popular and low-cost way to gain exposure to the stock market as a whole, rather than trying to pick individual stocks.

*Strategies for Managing Risk:*

- ➤ Diversify your portfolio across different asset classes, such as stocks, bonds, and real estate.
- ➤ Set clear investment goals and stick to a long-term plan, rather than making impulsive decisions based on short-term market fluctuations.
- ➤ Avoid investing more than you can afford to lose and maintain an emergency fund to cover unexpected expenses.
- ➤ Keep an eye on fees and expenses, which can eat into your returns over time.
- ➤ Consider using stop-loss orders to limit potential losses on individual stocks.
- ➤ Stay informed about market trends and developments but avoid reacting emotionally to daily market fluctuations.
- ➤ Regularly review your portfolio and adjust your investments as necessary to ensure that you remain on track to meet your financial goals.

## Additional resources for stock investing

Stock investing can be a complex and challenging field, and there are many resources available to help investors make informed decisions and manage their portfolios effectively. Here are a few resources that you may find helpful:

> Financial news and analysis websites: Websites such as Yahoo Finance, Bloomberg, and CNBC provide up-to-date news, analysis, and data on stocks, as well as tools for tracking your portfolio and conducting research.

> Online brokerages: Many online brokerages, such as Charles Schwab, Fidelity, and E-Trade, offer a range of resources and tools for investors, including research reports, market data, and educational materials.

> Investment newsletters: Investment newsletters such as The Motley Fool, Morningstar, and Barron's provide analysis and commentary on stocks and other investment vehicles, as well as recommendations and tips for investors.

> Investment books: There are countless books on investing, from classic texts such as Benjamin Graham's "The Intelligent Investor" to more recent works such as Ray Dalio's "Principles: Life and Work." Reading books on investing can provide valuable insights into the principles and strategies used by successful investors.

> Professional financial advisors: If you feel overwhelmed by the complexities of stock investing, or if you don't have the time or inclination to manage your own portfolio, consider working with a professional financial advisor. A good advisor can help you develop a personalized investment plan, provide guidance on managing risk, and help you stay on track to meet your financial goals.

> Online communities and forums: There are many online communities and forums where investors can connect, share ideas, and learn from each other. Examples include r/investing on Reddit, the Bogleheads forum, and the Stock Market Investing group on Facebook.

Remember, no single resource or strategy is guaranteed to lead to success in stock investing. It's important to do your own research, consider multiple perspectives, and make decisions based on your own goals, risk tolerance, and financial situation. With patience, discipline, and a commitment to ongoing learning, you can build a successful stock portfolio and achieve your long-term financial goals.

## FAQs and common misconceptions

Stock investing can be a complex and often confusing topic, with many misconceptions and questions surrounding it. In this section, we'll explore some common FAQs and misconceptions on stock investing to help you better understand this field.

**FAQs**

*What are stocks, and how do they work?*

Stocks represent ownership in a company, and their value is determined by the performance of the company and the overall market. When you buy stocks, you become a shareholder in the company and may be entitled to receive dividends or vote on important company decisions.

*How do I pick stocks to invest in?*

There are many strategies for picking stocks, including fundamental analysis (examining a company's financial statements and growth potential), technical analysis (studying charts and market data to identify trends and patterns), and index investing (investing in a broad range of stocks through index funds). It's important to do your own research and consider your own goals and risk tolerance before making any investment decisions.

*What is diversification, and why is it important?*

Diversification involves spreading your investments across a variety of stocks, industries, and asset classes to minimize the impact of any one stock or sector on your portfolio. Diversification can help reduce risk and volatility and improve long-term returns.

*How can I manage risk when investing in stocks?*

Managing risk involves diversifying your portfolio, setting clear investment goals, avoiding investing more than you can afford to lose, and staying informed about market trends and developments. It's also important to avoid reacting emotionally to short-term market fluctuations and to regularly review and adjust your portfolio as necessary.

*How much money do I need to start investing in stocks?*

There is no set amount of money required to start investing in stocks, and it's possible to start with as little as a few hundred dollars. However, it's important to have a clear understanding of your own financial situation and investment goals before investing any money.


**Common Misconceptions**

*Investing in stocks is gambling*

While there is always a degree of risk involved in investing in stocks, it is not the same as gambling. Investing involves careful research and analysis, a long-term strategy, and a willingness to accept risk and volatility. Unlike gambling, investing in stocks can generate long-term returns and build wealth over time.

*You need to be an expert to invest in stocks*

While it's important to do your own research and stay informed about market trends, you don't need to be an expert to invest in stocks. Many online resources, such as financial news websites, investment newsletters, and online brokerages, provide valuable tools and information for investors of all levels.

*Investing in individual stocks is always better than investing in index funds*

While individual stocks may offer the potential for higher returns, they also carry a higher degree of risk and require more research and management. Index funds, on the other hand, offer a diversified approach to investing in the stock market as a whole and can help minimize risk and volatility.

*Timing the market is the key to successful investing*

Trying to time the market or buying and selling stocks based on short-term market fluctuations, is a risky and often unsuccessful strategy. Instead, it's important to have a long-term investment plan and stick to a disciplined approach that takes into account your own goals and risk tolerance.

*Investing in stocks is only for the wealthy*

While it's true that some stocks require a high minimum investment, it's possible to invest in stocks with as little as a few hundred dollars. Many online brokerages also offer low-cost investing options, making it easier for people of all income levels to invest in stocks.

Stock investing can be a challenging and complex field, but with careful research and a disciplined approach, it can be a valuable way to build wealth over time. By diversifying your portfolio, setting clear investment goals, and staying informed about market trends and developments, you can manage risk and make informed investment decisions. Remember to be patient, avoid reacting emotionally to short-term market fluctuations, and focus on a long-term strategy that takes into account your own goals and risk tolerance. With these tips in mind, you can navigate the world of stock investing with confidence and success.

### Next steps and recommended reading

If you're interested in learning more about stock investing, there are many resources available to help you get started. Here are some recommended next steps and reading materials:

- ➢ Open a brokerage account - To begin investing in stocks, you'll need to open a brokerage account. There are many online brokerages available, each with its own set of fees, investment options, and tools. Do your research to find the one that's right for you.
- ➢ Read investing books - There are many excellent books available on the topic of stock investing, ranging from beginner-friendly introductions to advanced technical analysis guides. Some highly recommended titles include "The Intelligent Investor" by Benjamin Graham, "One Up On Wall Street" by Peter Lynch, and "The Little Book of Common Sense Investing" by John Bogle.
- ➢ Take an online course - Many online courses are available that cover the basics of stock investing, as well as more advanced topics like technical analysis and risk management. Some popular online courses include those offered by Coursera, Udemy, and Khan Academy.

- ➤ Follow financial news and blogs - Staying informed about market trends and developments is key to making informed investment decisions. Subscribe to financial news outlets like Bloomberg, CNBC, and The Wall Street Journal, as well as popular investing blogs like Seeking Alpha and The Motley Fool.
- ➤ Join investing forums - Joining online investing forums can be a great way to connect with other investors, share knowledge and experiences, and ask questions. Some popular investing forums include Reddit's r/investing and r/StockMarket, as well as online communities like the Bogleheads forum.

By taking these next steps and diving deeper into the world of stock investing, you can continue to grow your knowledge and make informed investment decisions. Remember to always do your own research, stay disciplined, and focus on your own investment goals and risk tolerance.

# About the author

The author of the book on stock investing is an experienced finance professional with a solid educational background. He obtained his bachelor's degree in engineering from a prestigious university and later pursued an MBA in finance. He also holds a CFA (Chartered Financial Analyst) charter, which is considered one of the most respected credentials in the finance industry.

The author's career in finance spans over two decades, during which he has gained extensive experience in various areas of finance. He began his career as an investment banker, where he worked on several high-profile deals and gained a deep understanding of financial markets and investment strategies. Over the years, he has held various positions in the finance industry, including as a financial analyst, valuation specialist and managing director of valuation of businesses and assets.

With his wealth of experience and knowledge, the author decided to write a book on stock investing to help people make better investment decisions. The book covers a wide range of topics, including the basics of stock investing, the different types of stocks, how to evaluate stocks, and how to build a diversified portfolio. It also provides practical tips and strategies for investors to maximize their returns while minimizing their risks.

Overall, the author is a highly accomplished finance professional with a passion for educating people about the benefits of stock investing. His book is a valuable resource for anyone looking to enter the world of stock investing and is highly recommended for both novice and experienced investors alike.